Steck-Vaughn Shutterbug Books SOCIAL STUDIES

That's Working Together!

by Susan Ring

STECK-VAUGHN
A Harcourt Company

www.steck-vaughn.com

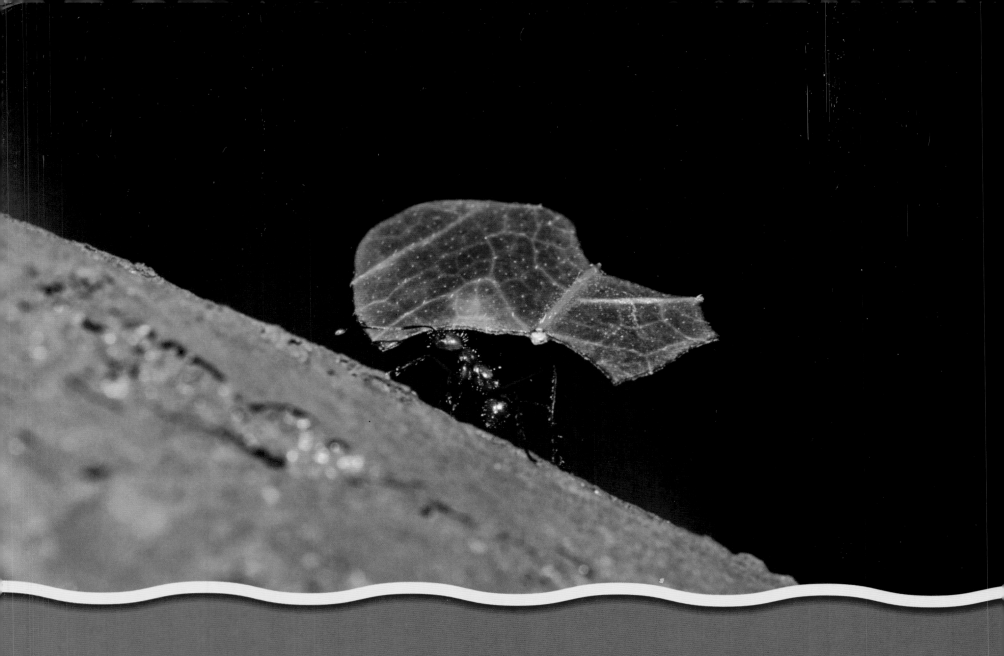

One ant can carry a leaf.

But it takes many ants to carry a lot of leaves.
That's working together!

What can two ants do?

One bee can get nectar from a flower.

Two ants can carry more leaves.

What can two bees do?

But it takes many bees to use nectar to make honey.
That's working together!

Two bees can get more nectar.

One person can build.

What can two people do?

But it takes many people to build a house.

That's working together!

Two people can build faster.

One person can cook dinner.

What can two people do?

But it takes many people to cook for a restaurant.
That's working together!

Two people can cook dinner faster.

One person can kick a ball.

What can two people do?

But it takes many people to play a soccer game.
That's working together!

Two people can kick a ball back and forth.

One person can paddle a boat.

What can two people do?

But it takes many people to paddle a boat really fast.
That's working together!

Two people can paddle a boat faster.

One person can help grapes grow.

What can two people do?

But it takes many people to pick a crop of grapes.
That's working together!

Two people can help pick grapes when they are ready.

Working together helps get things done.
Being part of a team can be so much fun!